PORTSMOUTH UNABRIDGED:
New Poems for an Old City

THE PORTSMOUTH POET LAUREATE PROGRAM

Edited by Maren C. Tirabassi

Photography by Richard Haynes

Peter E. Randall Publisher
Portsmouth, New Hampshire
2002

The Portsmouth Poet Laureate Program,
P. O. Box 1196, Portsmouth, New Hampshire, 03802.

Peter E. Randall Publisher
P. O. Box 4726, Portsmouth, NH, 03802
www.PERPublisher.com

Distributed by University Press of New England
    Hanover and London

Design: Deidre Randall

Library of Congress: Cataloging-in-Publication data

Portsmouth unabridged: new poems for an old city: the Portsmouth
Poet Laureate Program/edited by Maren C. Tirabassi; photography by
Richard Haynes.
    p.cm.
    ISBN 1-931807-06-X
1. American poetry—New Hampshire—Portsmouth. 2. City and town
life—Poetry. 3. Portsmouth (N.H.)—Poetry. I. Tirabassi, Maren C. II.
Haynes, Richard., 1949- III. Portsmouth Poet Laureate Program.
    PS549.P8 P68 2002
    811'.508097426—dc21

                                                            2002001780

Poems which have appeared elsewhere:
Rodger Martin, "Sailing Past Portsmouth Naval Prison to The Isles of
Shoals," *Sahara* Fall/Winter, 2000 and *WEVO's What's Your Story.* John
Perrault, "The Tugs," in *Soundings East*, 1989. Esther Buffler, "Black
Night" in *String of Pearls.* Marie Harris, "G is for Gundalow" in *A New
Hampshire Alphabet Book* (Sleeping Bear Press, Chelsea, MI 2002).
Elizabeth Knies, "The Mourning Dove," in *White Peonies* in the Oyster
River Press chapbook series, *Walking to Windward.* Katherine E.
Solomon, "Accidental Light" in *Baybury Review*, spring/summer, 1998.

Porstsmouth Unabridged: New Poems for an Old City is supported in part
by a grant from the New Hampshire State Council on the Arts and by
the National Endowment for the Arts, as well as by a grant from the
Greater Piscataqua Community Foundation.

CONTENTS

WE'RE ALL TOURISTS IN TIME

IN THE NEIGHBORHOODS

ILLUSTRATIONS

Brief Introduction and Warm Appreciation

Site-specific poetry—spiritual cartography, verbal landscape, writing with place—is perhaps the most invitational poetic form. A poet who shares the home-place of memoir or the impact-moment of travel-writing acknowledges that an integral part of any life encounter is the place where it takes place. Site-specific poetry is vivid with sights, sounds, smells, with the taste of saltwind or coffee, new-caught fish or "two with the works", with the texture of stone whale, tide pool brown rockweed tracings, curled seafarers' maps, free movie theatre dishes.

Today I look out my window and through the Januarybare hedges I see the beautiful house that my neighbor Louise has re-built with such care, the crimson feathers of a cardinal finding last berries, and the Lafayette Road early morning high school traffic. Where you read this book will offer a different perspective. When you read it, you will find ninety-two unique perspectives on the city of Portsmouth. Feel free to take off your shoes!

Those who have contributed to *Portsmouth Unabridged* are as diverse as the city itself. The Portsmouth Poet Laureate Program has been lifting up poetry in a wide range of settings for the last five years. From Frames to Festival, from local Hoot to World Poetry Forum, the Working Group has made poetry central to our community. Richard Haynes, photographer, "light-writer", who has served on the Poet Laureate Selection Committee, was the genius behind connecting visual and verbal images. The gift of Richard's work on *Portsmouth Unabridged* has opened a new aperture for artistic collaboration. And the poets, ranging in age from nine to one hundred years, who submitted their individual work have been an amazing group with whom to shape a manuscript more interesting than any one of us could have imagined.

Financial support for *Portsmouth Unabridged* has come from grants by the New Hampshire State Council on the Arts, the National Endowment for the Arts, and the Greater Piscataqua Community Foundation, as well as donations from a host of local businesses listed on our bookmark. Gratitude also goes to businesses and individuals whose consistent contributions sustain the ongoing activities of the Portsmouth Poet Laureate Program.

The City of Portsmouth has offered enthusiasm and encouragement to the Portsmouth Poet Laureate Program since its inception. How grateful we are to live in a community which recognizes and values the arts.

Facilitating particular aspects of this project have been poet Diana Durham, in a residency with educator Millie Parks at the New Franklin School and poet Hildred Crill who, with Kristin Forselius of Artists In Residence, brought high school students to the Button Factory to write about the visual arts of Darlene Furbush Oulette and Bonney Goldstein. Anne Dewees and Mimi White used oral history techniques to share stories of an earlier Portsmouth. New Heights graciously hosted the workshop, "All Over the Map—Writing with Place". Thanks goes to educators Kelli Maynard of Portsmouth Middle School and John Ferguson of Exeter High School for coordinating poetry submissions by some of their gifted student writers.

My daughter Maria Tirabassi contributed hours of editorial assistance as well as typing this entire manuscript in preparation to giving it to Peter and Deidre Randall who handle every project they publish with the sensitivity, skill and grace that turns scattered ideas and fragile possibilities into that wonderful creation ... a book!

And then, of course, there is "thanks" to Portsmouth itself—the restaurants where poets sat to write, the Square and Memorial Bridge—real characters in several poems, the Piscataqua river banks and neighborhood streets, the texture of history still visible and the energy of a future yet to be realized. Some of the *Portsmouth Unabridged* poets were born in Portsmouth; some live here now; some have been visitors. All were startled and changed by this "old city" with its many moods. This volume offers their "new poems", confident that there will be many more images—written with words and, yes, Richard, written with light.

Maren C. Tirabassi
Portsmouth Poet Laureate 2001-2003

Welcome to Portsmouth

Parking Garage

Crumbling, unsound structure,
Reeking of motor oil, gas fumes.
(Relief still, to find a space.)
Then —
Revelation:
On these walls
Words
From a different dimension
Stirring, moving, concise.
Stay here.

Josephine Hughes

Breaking New Grounds

The Haven

I was already anticipating my destination,
    or, at least, my immediate destination;
    for where I was headed in the longer run
    was far less certain, but equally as enticing.
But for now, I knew where I wanted to go.
It would be comfortable there,
    a place which enveloped you
    like a favorite old sweater you'd put on
    to wrap yourself in contentment,
    a place where familiarity brought
    a calm which needn't be questioned.
I was there at the door,
    greeted by hospitality for the senses.
The Sight of the walls laden with beverage choices, artwork,
    a display case full of desserts.
The Sound of talking, of quiet,
    of a machine's mechanical whirring,
    perfecting the substance for which this place is known.
The Smell of warmth or of coolness, as dictated by the seasons,
    of subtle flavors combining, creating, enticing.
The Taste of the nectar which flows freely
    and draws us here.
The Touch of the welcoming,
    the calmness that surrounds you,
    the feeling of freedom to be alone
    and yet be part of the whole,
    part of the world of this place.
It felt good; this is where I needed to be,
    and it helped me realize that
    despite the flux of life and the world in general,
    there is a right direction,
    a place to move on towards,
    an existence to strive for.
There really is something to be said about
    Breaking New Grounds.

Tris A. Motyl

Zaatar Café

We come once a month on a Wednesday
to this meeting place for gourmet coffee,
rare, exotic teas, some poetry, singers of songs
whose words lap at the shore
of somewhere in particular,
prairie-light which will
carry the evening.

One poet talks about Rilke's
"Self-Portrait," and I try one:
"Right eyelid curves over eyeball
as if to ask for sleep."
Green tea chai, words rise
with the steam, someone dreams audibly
while pebbles drop inside Zaatar's—
this rain stick of poets—gathered.

Karen Nelson

Emilio Wins Again

He's not trying to get rich just trying to make a living
A way with words is a gift he's been given
Emilio's the man who's making my lunch
And Linda's in the kitchen she's backing him up

He's got beans that are hot and beans that are cold
They've got more flavor than beans have ever known
He makes the food his Mama used to make
And seldom will you find a tourist in the place

He'll see you through the week or he'll see you through the window
Tell him where you're from 'cause he might speak your lingo
He takes cash and he gives advice
It's a bargain no matter what the price

He gets smaller as he's walking away
He's a master of having something to say
He's a minimalist of the truest kind
Painting little pictures one plate at a time

The counter is the canvas the food is the art
Give the man some room the show's about to start
He makes it look easy but we know it's not
'Cause no one else has what he's got

If you want it right now come back later and get it
Good food takes time but you won't regret it
If your cell phone's ringing he'll let you know
That you're too busy and you've got to go

Emilio wins again

Emilio wins again

It's nice to see nice people.

Mickey Blanchette

At Joe's Pizza

I have the delivery guy's home number, know where he lives,
know his headlights. It gets so quiet at Joe's Pizza, you could hear
a plastic fork drop. If it's a puff of flour, time enough for my fingers

to pick away at the crust. A speck of sauce, just a single paper napkin
to wipe the corners of my mouth. Here, across the street from the row
of store windows filled with mannequins in wedding gowns, the test

of everything is simply this: I noticed the world was getting fatter.
I was chewing on a slice of pepperoni with extra cheese.
Nearby, a boy in stained shirt was wiggling his toes playing

this little piggy goes to the market and so on. An old woman, with globes
for eyes, slapped the hand of a bubble gum machine away from the trash.
It was on a day like today. I was licking my chops trying to decide

over hazelnut or tiramisu, while a black sock in a black boot
stood at attention waiting to take my order. Behind the glass counter
lives the grim telephone that never stops ringing, pizza boxes stacked tall

like sky scrapers pitched against the night, and the cook who pounds out
dough with her fists, then cuts a piping hot pie to pieces. Such opulence
lives on the lips of the oven boy, the world's shirt hanging out of its
    trousers.

Andrew Howe

Joe's Pizza

Home, and its Opposite

Paris, that Bastille day:
sunshine and egg crêpes on the Left Bank
and playing bluegrass in the Metro
just long enough to earn our beer money
before the gendarmes tell us to move along
like the cops told us to move along
as we tried vainly to earn our beer money
singing Jacques Brel ditties
and stomping our feet to keep warm
that First Night, in Portsmouth.

Andrew C. Periale

First Night

I, the swan of blue ice
all the places like Reykjavik
locked in the arctic, and you,
the boat laden with salt from Iona,
the white heat of Greece, are trapped
in the moonbeam, our shadows dancing
on tug boats. I whisper a mixture of umlauts and accents,
melt me, oh, melt me, my skin weeps, melt me. After the fireworks,
wings in puddles, I'll crawl to the sea to climb your hull
red-bellied with rust, tarred and unleaking, lapping
and slapping and sloughing away.

Patricia L. Frisella

First Night

Midnight rolls over and falls upon us.
Standing in a parking lot freezing
the fireworks flag down the oncoming year
with tremendous vigor,
while doing little to suppress the hypothermia
taking over my body.
But soon after those airborne chemical reactions
comes the sulfuric stench
which burns the collective olfactory nerve
as it douses the crowd
and engulfs the ball park,
while we had lost interest
and threw smoke bombs under cars.
Much more enthralled with our own reckless actions
than those of the pyrotechnicians
while the cheers of the crowd rattle
the workings of the metallic bleachers.
Happy new year, Happy century,
welcome to the future.

Zachary Cranor

Caffé Kilim

The Bench Outside Caffé Kilim

Spring sunsets can bring a cold, angry wind
Or a warm cloak of humid air
That settles on the city like a shroud

Tonight is like that, warm and thick
And laden with fog and mist

The sky burns a brilliant red
And a cracked mosaic
Of thin cloud cover fragments the light
Revealing infinite subtleties of hue
Sun devils dance across the fractured rainbow
As the warm wetness descends upon the streets

From the Northeast, a sink of low pressure
Pregnant with moisture from the Gulf of Maine
Spins across the rocky coastline
Leaves, buds, goldenrod and tall grass sparkle
In celebration of the arrival of the dew

And as night falls in Portsmouth
The city lights do the same

Chris Elliott

At Café Brioche

Plath's hoof-taps echo down the parking garage, across the street
to the counter where I stand, so much from the world
in front of me—baguettes, boursin, croquembouche,
and *chevre*, a man tells a woman, *French for sheep.*
Sheep or goat. Same thing. Wildflowers on tablecloths, just visible. I dwell
on how unequivocal, more reliable than sprigs floating near Christ's face
across the Shroud of Turin. That and the French words, Sisters of the
 Visitation,
behind screens in cloisters, rise up and I recite "La Ballade des Pendus,"
or some of it, watching headless Chocolate Custard Nuns, carpe diem
 espresso,
white demitasses lined up on the trash barrel. Hand light on my shoulder,
a woman turns her face to mine, says *Jackie? No. Someone else.*
The Portuguese I try melts into French, to Latin, as I write
to someone in Santarém, Pará, wanting to tell him how I came to this café
once with blood splattered on my arms. He wrote to me
the story of a child who *dreams of being a bird but gets no answer,*
wakes up, seeing the town in flying. She asks, what can I do
for my town? Visions in his letter that I can't hold onto
rise and are lost across a large sky. I will embroider this tablecloth
with spirals, crosses, more wildflowers—permanent
as the intricacies of the wrought iron chair I sit on,
what I always hope to remember, but cannot.

Hildred Crill

Pick Up ?

Late spring day
outside café
hazelnut coffee
beside pen and
paper

I try to
capture moments
as I always
do

Disheveled
unshaved
he stopped to
ask my plans
for the day

Disappeared
into a crowd
when I mentioned
meeting a
friend

Sasha Wolfe

Rusty Hammer

Salt on the wind, the foghorn calling across town—
I watched your hands circle a beer in a booth
at the Rusty Hammer, thinking these narrow streets
could not hold us. New England windows, fluid
as water, guide me to the harbor. Lips chilled
by moonlight, I search for crows who gather by the hundreds
over Market Square and find the words we spoke that day
hanging shyly above the steeple. We have become historians, eating
from the red and blue of painted plates, politely asking for sugar
in crazy rooms with slanted floors. We did not paint these walls,
we were given forest green, mud brown by pilgrims
who buried pot shards in the back yard with broken pipes
and the soles of high-laced shoes. You can hear their carriages
still, the tap of horse on cobblestone; you can find their hats
and tea cups behind the cemetery. Gulls keening over the rooftops—
this canopy bed is none I recognize, though I seem
to know the spider crossing the wall. *I come from a long line*
of careful souls, you told me, your face reflected
in polished wood, the weekend crowd cheering a football
game over the bar. *Teachers and farmers, maintenance men,*
women baking Indian pudding and pumpkin bread.
The Memorial Bridge is rimmed in ice tonight and the crows
have gone wherever it is they sleep. The lights shut down
in the Rusty Hammer, lining the street in black glass.
On a fog-laced afternoon neither of us gave an answer.
We buttoned our coats and left a tip for the blonde
in a tight tee shirt, following the ancestors
across the square.

Katherine Towler

Rusty Hammer

Black Night

(of the Rockingham)

Now the night wind begins.
And I am alone. It is black night.
Spits of ice pit-pit into the chimney
like patterns of print in sound.
I listen to the frailness
in each dropping of sleet

like the trapped bird's crystal chirp
caught in the wet chimney of the
bayed room. Waiting out winter's end,
I urge myself to move, speak.
But there is no fire tonight
in this unlit space.

Esther Buffler

In Wal-Mart

Rusted wellbuckets swarm its granite lawn,
bumping and slamming into each other, like
young male bulls, fighting for dominance.
Visitors approach,
dodging the bulging
spring water from the silver bells.
Bursting through the resisting doors,
they become customers,
searching for the Holy Grail.
But in the end each customer,
visitor loses sight of treasure.
Pockets empty,
they turn back,
back into the night
with nothing and alone.

Hunter Hideriotis

Pink Granite Benches

South Church Unitarian has new pink benches
Cold stone, but solid and time worthy
I wait for a concert, admiring volunteer gardens
where weeds have suffocated flowers,
one young boy tugs on a mom
Making one last cellular call,
Missing a chance for her voice
To matter in her
son's life
The pink granite benches sit cold and firm...waiting

Nancy B. Knapp

In Town

A sunny day
A stroll in town, my friend and I
Bakery to bakery to bakery
Warm, crusty bread to fill our families
Talk, laughter to fill our souls.

So many choices
We lunch, and after
Steaming mugs, chocolate cookies
What a perfect café seat!

We sit
Watching people watching people
Soon we'll go
But not now
One more cup
And ask no more of this resplendent Portsmouth day.

Julie Doherty

North Church as seen from the Atheneaum.

Play

I stroll "Downtown"—
as it is contemporarily called—
to converse with the actors congregating outside of North Church.
They are already costumed for their roles of stoners, slackers, sages,
and perform with a tragic alacrity
having rehearsed exhaustively for a lifetime of performances.

It is against my better judgment that I find my mark in this small
    town repertory,
yet I cannot halt my feet as they tap out a rhythm of
derision
deprecation
disdain
in harmony with this masquerade.

The scenery erected is antique,
its clapboard and brick serve as fronts
for life.
The atmosphere infuses me as I edge closer to the action—
I am soaked with a vibrancy of spring
although I can taste metallic autumn creeping up on the crowd.

In the midst of painted faces,
I am obtrusively ordinary.
Familiarities are flung over my head
as I stand by—
a non-participatory audience member
of Downtown charades.

Maria I. Tirabassi

One Day in One Life

A bright light tells me to move.
As I weave through the sea of people,
I smell steak grilling and saltwater.
Some things always stay the same.
The ground uneven beneath my feet
keeps my senses sharp and my walk nimble.
I pass by some people with
dark clothes, markings on their bodies,
and a cloud of curling smoke.
When I was younger,
I would distance my body from them,
as if their looks could harm me.
Now I smile and nod.
I receive a few back.
This town harbors what we need
to carry on. Difference.
And that's what makes me walk on
to another day.

Adrian E. Carney

An American Poem No One Should Have To Write

From an iron wrought bench surrounded by
begonias and tidy bricks on the most
beautiful of evenings in a town where
the ships are always in and the salt falls
like the best of memories, I saw him.
Walking too fast through the theater crowd
now milling outside Cafe Brioche
with their mocha and cinnamon coffees.
It wasn't his loose clothing or unshaven
face, or even his unkempt hair
that stopped me. It was his shoes. Canvas
and holes. But ragged holes that made me think
of rats and rusting pipes, abandoned rails.
A place a city leaves underground
when it decides to change direction.
A place where water doesn't drip anymore,
it ticks behind forgotten walls.
And I just knew—an American poem
should never, ever have to come to this.

S. Stephanie

I sit and listen to the gory details
of a death I didn't see,
a man I never knew

reputedly kind
reportedly handsome

I sit and think
of the way our lives
almost intertwined

a man I didn't know
a block from where I work,
the hardwood floor I walk on
the espresso machines I use

Portsmouth is a small town
I could have passed him
beaten
and the beat goes on
the conversation changes
the beans roll and the snow falls down
and the cars I'll never
ride in pass me by.

Jessie Bellantone

No More Wallflowers (For Jeannie From PASS)

When the tall girl walks in on stilts she has built,
her head blooming, her eyes popping, her silver
danceshoes glued flipflops studded with stars,
I roll over like the dog I am
and lick her high, high heels.

When the tall girl swishes in taffeta,
or chenille, I paint roses on the moon
with my tongue.

When the tall girl sashays, ambles,
lollygags down the hall,
I chase her wake, sniff and pant,
just for a whiff of her ankles,
her pungent weather.

I say when the tall girl glides in,
under my skin, pushes right in,
I freeze,
and my breath goes staccato.

I say when this bad girl shows up,
her purse swinging, her hips tossing,
her platinum hair like a global helmet
I'd just love to peel off.

I say when she swims on air,
pressing her chest through
this dark place, scheming.

When she turns,
slicing and craning,
back at you,
you'll be wrapped and chewed,
though nothing will save you

when the tall girl chooses and she chooses you.

Mimi White

Reality (after the work of Darlene Furbush Oullett)

I sit here
staring...

I sit here
listening...

I sit here
knowing...

knowing nothing
but reality
what's right there
in front of me

I see the paintings
before me

wishing I could stand up
and jump right into

the dream world
which is much too close
for comfort
but yet
still far beyond my reach

wishing that I could make
what I see mine
for me and no one else
a place to escape to
a place to be alone
a place I could change
as quickly as I choose
with one single stroke of
a brush
with one lonely color

I can see

this world
only in the far reaches
of my imagination
if only I could feel my
dream world
with the tips of my fingers,
if only I could
smudge the near dry
paint.

Katyanne Kinneavy

In Her Studio (after the work of Bonney Goldstein)

Through red cracked paint on the window panes
the rain pitter pats on the glass
and the tar on the street three stories below
while inside the artist's work is
never finished, never ending
just like the constant weather
outside the cracked painted windows.

As the wind blows
and the stars come out the artist
packs up for the evening.

Jessica Meadowcroft

To Market, To Market

Streaking through the crowds in Market Square
Excites the curiosity of those
Who need the false security of clothes
Or envy those of us who travel bare.

Police Chief Russ has cleared the thoroughfare
So Congress Street, where traffic usually goes,
Has us with nothing on from heads to toes,
Running unburdened through the morning air.

The library was next, it's moved? No fair.
Not yet, it hasn't gone, no spot's been chose.
We ask Mike Huxtable because he knows
Where books are shelved that cover subjects bare.

Paul Jones salutes us at Haymarket Square;
We had not yet begun to run. We're loose!
We run down Richards Ave. and Griffin's goose
Sees us so cleanly plucked its nostrils flare.

Hospital Hill, my children born up there;
The causeway that is lined with wild rose
And ragweed that provokes the springtime nose.
The South Mill Pond reflects our bodies fair.

We turn and run into a Pleasant stare.
Through traffic lights that change where nothing goes.
In Market Square we find our empty clothes
And cover up our souls with what we wear.

John Ferguson

Part, Body, and Soul

Part...
I'm working on the old red wagon,
Putting it back together once more.
When all at once the project's draggin';
Missing a part, it's happened before.

I begin by looking all over town;
A part that old; it won't be easy.
It's where I should have started, down
At that Portsmouth legend, Peavey's.

Body...
Now, of course, my stomach is growling.
I look at my watch; it's past lunchtime.
Way too hungry to do much prowling,
I long for hot dogs and chili sublime.

There's no need, I think, to delay so,
For it's there, as the nose on my face.
For hot dogs and chili, you always go
Behind the garage, to Gilley's place.

and Soul...
The conversation in Gilley's is great:
The Bruins, the Red Sox, the mayor.
It's time to go, before it's too late,
For that soul food beyond compare.

A couple of blocks, or is it three?
I must hurry before it gets dark,
To sights and smells of flowers and sea,
To the spirit-filling Prescott Park.

Francis Robert Morris

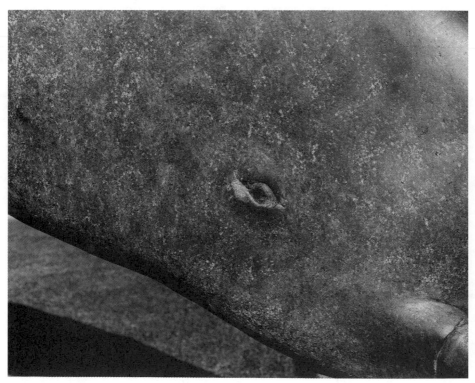

Whale's face

The Whale in Prescott Park

Awed by the glistening gray-black
Power that looked like it had emerged
Moments ago from the sea.
So smooth and massive was this creature
Of the dark depths of water.
Allowing me, only me
To adventure through aquatic worlds
Or lounge upon its great back.
Fantasy fades, away I totter
To the comfort of mother.
Upon return, everything is small
To a no longer tiny girl's eyes.
Innocent wonder smothered
By experience, fear, growing pain.
Where was the ocean's grand king
That enthralled a child's mystic dreams?
I recoil in surprise
At the shadow of magnificence.
No more than a few feet tall
Dark brother of Ahab's phantom white
No longer tremendous
My imagination, out of steam,
Stares blankly at the once whale
Now just a statue, my vision stale.

Meghan Haslam

The Path of the Piscataqua

G is for Gundalow

This rugged sailing barge, steady and slow,
Hauled without number
Bricks, apples, lumber
Down from the farms to the city below.

Marie Harris

The Piscataqua river from aboard the Thomas Leighton

Reggae on the River

It's a long summer tradition
among rastas, and people who remember
the Caribbean, to find
live-vibe, drink down rum, and swing
the body from the pelvis.
Anonymous on the Thomas Leighton,
astride the Portsmouth shoreline,
aglitter in the early evening,
we regard our city from behind.

The band tunes up.
"Danny Tucker and the Vibe Tribe",
ska toonin', Marley-croonin',
icons to music followers,
who map their summers
on the chance to dance on a boat,
in the moon, under stars,
on the river, out to sea.

We stretch summer to the
ten mile limit –
the Isles of Shoals run,
delivering the water supply,
watching the lanternlit line
of chapel goers up the crest
of Star,

while we return to shore,
tequila consumed, unhinged hips
scoring rhythm to the bone,
on a dance floor balanced
on the ocean,
with those who keep dancing,
playing, and sailing us out to sea.

Kate Leigh

Memorial Bridge

I like watching the boats
and I don't mind the traffic
except when a really heavy truck goes over me.

I hate it when they lift my middle up.
I feel like putty that's just been stretched in the center.

I connect Portsmouth to Maine,
what would they do if it wasn't for me?

I like warm summer evenings when
the buoy and city lights turn on.
It's nice to talk to my friend Sarah Long,
she lives next door.

It's a big treat when they give me a new
layer of paving,
it feels like a warm blanket is being draped
over me.
The only part I don't like is when the cement and construction
pave over my head.
It sounds as if a waterfall is smashing next to my ear
and a hammer is pounding right above me.

I can see the Piscataqua River and the
John Wanamaker Restaurant.
The water shimmers in the moon
and glistens in the sun.
That's my life!

Jacob Bender

Three Scenes by the River

Morning, small apartment with coffee:

To smooth a small scar on her left cheek
gloss her auburn hair
lubricate the ragged purr of her cat
a cod yields his liver

Noon, the Puddledock:

Silvering the dark surface
and disappearing, animal or sparkle?
in the old wharf's slat light
flashes of fingerlings

Night, Memorial Bridge facing SE:

Salt-scarred dory cleaves
in half on the inbound tide
late summer bluefish moon on the river
liquid stars waver under her
hair untucked from behind her ear
swims in the eddy of her face
tickles her nose and eyelid
her back to the fish-licked breeze

Rick Agran

N.H. Summer

She loved the rocks and scrubby pastures,
New Hampshire, the sea always nearby.

Wild young child running on the rough gray beach
lifts eyes, hoping for the clouds to unveil the sun.

Night coming, sand cold and damp beneath her feet,
she resentfully turns to go home.

She welcomes the warmth of her bed and
wonders when the tide will chase itself out.

By morning, a treasure of shells and stones —
innocent summer of her childhood.

JudyAnn Yudkin

While the Bridge is Up ...or... Portsmouth on a Bridge

With the mist so thick
you'd think we were
living in the clouds.
Though I suppose that
in Heaven
there aren't such inconveniences as
waiting in line.
Still
it's quite pleasant actually.
Window unrolled
dampness strokes my face like fingers
and the smell of the sea makes me hungry
for oysters
and cold Smuttynose beer.

The tugboats hoot at one another across the mist
rhythmic cooing

I slip into a silky fog of my own.
A hazy stew of thoughts
what to wear who to call
what to be how to feel
who to love who to hate
where to go when to go what to do when I get there
sleep in late or get up early
put my money in the bank or spend it all
to laugh to cry to imagine the worst imagine the best
to have a coke a beer stick to water
go to Chile stay at home
cut my hair keep it long
believe in God adopt a cat
fall in love or stay alone.

Faint outline of the ship
(hazy ghost ship)
massive
full of steel and parts.
People leave their cars
and
like children
lean over the edge for
a better look.

It is past the hour.
I will be late
(late again)
but
"The bridge was up" I will say
and roll my eyes
as if those boat people had a lot of nerve sailing through
just as I was about to cross.
I will pretend to be annoyed
but really I am
(secretly)
a little pleased.

Hillary W. Smith

Portsmouth Naval Prison

Sailing Past Portsmouth Naval Prison to The Isles of Shoals

Icon of MacBeth, edifice to maim the Piscataqua,
muscling up millennia like a whiskey-whizzened
sailor demanding rehabilitation, how many
battered souls chiselled letters in the iron grates
of your past? How many thousands lined the bars,
strained for a glimpse of beauty aboard this daily ferry?
How many sought salvation from Christians or Homers
who burst out here to the boiling edge of Smuttynose?
How many prayed for deep-throated combers to deliver them
from the cold? It is easy to suffer this protocol quietly,
look back on the main and pretend, but the sentences
of waves, those wind-sent court orders, each a crock and brace
of memory, lie with the heavy slap and wash of place
from that which we come to there which we go.

Rodger Martin

Fishing at the Shoals

Launched at Great Bay Marina
Going full throttle to get out of there fast
Wind whipping your hair and tears in your eyes
From going so fast
It's just my dad, my uncle, my little cousin, and I
It's a hot, sunny day perfect for fishing
There are lots of boats out there including
Two charter boats
One which my dad worked on when he was younger
Sun glistening on the water
Trolling for Blues
The thrill of hearing the words "FISH ON"
Rods bending, line going out
It's hard reeling in
It's awesome fighting big Blues
We land fifteen fish that day
Going full throttle back in before the sun sets
What a perfect day of fishing

Jake Hathaway

Treasure Hunting on Star Island

My brothers and I were pirates once
on broken rocks, rockweed under-
foot. Picking through shells and seaweed,
overturning rocks, looking for a rusted
nail, an encrusted coin, or driftwood
once whittled with a cutlass.

Instead, across heath, a beardless man, swinging stick
as gulls turn cloudless summer sky gray.
"They're just eggs," he says, leaning on yoke
stained stick, "too many here. Too populated
for the tourists."

Moving back toward the ship, toward the summer
houses, Captain Kidd's treasure is still under rock-
weed hidden where only gulls know.

Michael Moore

Monuments, Star Island

I wind through berry, rose, and poison ivy
to a small clearing with a towering obelisk:
lengthy praise high chiseled into stone
for the Rev. John Tucke. Past this monument
the path rises, then opens
onto a seaward chop of barren, fractured rock.
Ahead, a precise pillar erected
for Captain John Smith
who tried to name these islands for himself.

Stepping along the margin of stone and scrub,
I find a hollow—a tiny graveyard
bound by wall and lilac:
three markers,
like curved headboards,
and a short, worn column
for the Beebe girls:

Jessie, Milly, and Mitty,
ages 2, 4 , and 7,
dead in springtime, 1863.
I trace the column's words
now smudged
with pumpkin colored lichen:
Millie's prayer,
*...Please Jesus take me
to the Lighted Place...,*
and Mitty's sigh,
*I don't want to die but
I'll do just as Jesus wants me to.*
The lines for Jessie
are unreadable.
Perhaps she just said,
Rock me, Daddy.

Lora Moore

Magic

A summer evening's light
fades in Prescott Park,
the crowd awaits the performance,
while children dance and cartwheel on the grass
near the black stone whale.

In through the gate nearest the pier
flows a collection of folks from a group home.

Tommy, with Down's Syndrome,
stands out amongst his peers.

He wears a bright beanie-copter cap,
carries a wooden wand with gold star on top,
and he bestows on those who pass within reach,
with all the grace and solemnity
of a parish priest at a christening,
a silent blessing, that only he can know.

And out on the river, the sailboat, Blackbird,
all sails reefed,
just in from Smuttynose,
motors in lazy pirouettes —

waiting

waiting

Tommy turns,
raises the gold star wand,
arms outstretched in anticipation,
dips it,
three times slowly, to the west.

The siren sounds,
Memorial Bridge lifts its bulk,
the Blackbird slips beneath to a safe harbor—

And Tommy's smile, that triumphant smile,
lights up the park as no klieg lights
ever
could.

Neil English

Moonlight with Reflection
(after the work of Darlene Furbush Oullett)

This painting is far away. It has a lot
of color to it. I can imagine myself
floating from the place. The breeze
blows my hair just like in winter
when it is really cold. The summer
has come. I can see it in the
moonlight with the reflection on the
water. In the mountains in the back
I can see all sorts of different colors
like blues, greens, and whites and
how they are linked together is
incredible, also how the mountains
have a purple shade and how they
are rolling in the background. In the
sky there are all sorts of different
colors. How the clouds sit there, float
by and how they even out. It
probably takes place out in the wild
far, far out. It smells like something
nice and sweet just like how you are.

Sarah Arlin

Seagull

Seagulls vs. Cormorants

I would love to be one hundred percent proud of the seagull,
so common at this pleasant confluence of river and sea.
It is always so impeccably dressed,
buttoned up, sartorially elegant, colors well defined,
black, gray, and smashing white.

But even when full of unfrocked clams,
crushed by dropping from on high (a stroke of avian wit)
the gull's voice
remains ever a whining, irrational complaint.
I lose my patience. Gulls chill my heart.

But the Northern Double Crested Cormorant,
not at all endowed by Nature,
seemingly devoid of interest in appearance,
rusty black with no relieving colors,
always drying its laundry, flapping its wings
standing almost upright —/

The cormorant does not complain.
He has a sense of humor, a philosophical bent.
Gaiety resides in every drab feather.
I like that in birds.

Joann Lipshires

My dad and I are heading out to sea.
We are going lobster fishing.
We have just passed the Piscataqua River bridge; the buoys are going up
and down like dolphins in the sea.
We pass the Peirce Island pool;
it is really crowded.
The waves are getting rough.
"Hey, I think there's a storm at sea," hollers my father.
We see a pack of heavy and terrifying clouds ahead.
The seagulls are taking cover,
but everyone knows a fisherman always stays out to get what he needs.

Drip...Drop...Plop!
I feel water dripping from the sky.
Drip...Drop...Drip,
The drops are starting to come down fiercely now.
"We will go home after three trawls," shouts my dad.
The waves are acting up...
Splash!
I get as wet as the fish in the water.
I'm not feeling well...
Blat!
We come home with forty-three lobsters to sell, and a bag full of... well,
you know.

Alison Rahn

Riverwalk

Fluid is the restless river flowing
That moves like a sleek cat in the night.
Its dark eyes glint back a faint sparkling
Discernible even in the dim light.
Flickering in among the trees
The wanderings reflecting
The potency of its stamina: self-made and free.
Gracefully balanced, its eyes stare
Freezing ice cold in a river of despair.
In the wake of its padded paw tracks left,
Turn and turn about, the river's theft
Following the scent of a kill.
Stealing swiftly, yet not quite still
The agile body moves with a powerful will.
Respected, proud, and fearless,
Nature's own possess no less.
Dignified and aloof, the river level stands,
With a resolve of its own, lapping up the land.
Just when you think the river is gone,
Unsuspectingly the phenomenon,
Like a cat of nine lives, springs back living on.
Cascading over stones,
Searching for new places to roam,
Following the waterway known to the ages,
It will eventually evaporate in the air in stages
Finding its own way home
Piscataqua.

Marsha Pelletier

Cranes

This was to be my saviour
city. A seeming lifetime of
boxes and lives in boxes in
cars in houses or apartments in
offices huddled over boxes
moving boxes cardboard
boxes car boxes came to
a halt
I learned to pronounce
Piscataqua
I learned to walk outside to
greet and be greeted
why yes this is
a city street with people you know
and don't know on it so
when my three years were up
and the boxes came for me again
I said no.

A seeming lifetime later I
looked up, just yesterday,
for something to remember
in case I had to leave be
cause boxes are sometimes less
scary than streets.

They didn't pop out at me
right away, not in a group, though
I had noticed them singly
here and
across the river, brontosauri by
day, red-eyed dragons at
night. I never saw them move.
However they must bend their
long necks, some wee morning hour,
because they rise up not with bogweed or Saint George
dangling, but bedecked with Merry Christmas.

Darby Tench

Piscataqua Fog

They are nights like these
   that I miss
      when I journey to drier places
Nights when the fogs sifts
   its way through
      the long needle fingers
        of pines
      rolling lazily up the Piscataqua
Nights when form is usurped
   by shadow
   and light is diffracted
     into vague pools
       in the water-heavy air
Enveloped in the smell of the sea
   in its changing tide
       sitting still on its haunches
     beneath an ethereal bank
     of wandering vapor
From somewhere in the shifting mists
   the tender skittering of one
      single
       leaf
  as it journeys
    almost noiselessly
      from tree to ground
The breath draws slowly the soft air
     as much water as oxygen
        as though the lungs could store it away
          for some journey to come
        when they burn for Piscataqua fog

Kara Douglas

Sanders Lobster Pound

Tide's Out by Sanders Lobster Pound

Blue heron stands on stick-like leg.
Its foot in mud and muck. The other
tucked, obscured within a feathery
garb of blue.
The tide is out, far out, and all I see
is what collects on any ocean floor
along the busy line of shore.
A lobster crate of wood, long past use,
feathery green from watery mold
where barnacles have found a home.
The morning mist hangs heavy
mingling with the fragrance of
lobsters steaming in huge vats —
essence sweeter than perfume.
I breathe in deep its richness,
a feasting for the soul.
The heron, too, patient, still, feasts
on surfacing crabs. The fog soon lifts.
The tide rolls in, with healing waters
covering in blue the ocean floor, and
toward the skies, blue on blue,
the heron flies.

Rose Marie Devoucoux

The Tugs

Up river
three harbor tugs
nose a crippled tanker
majestic with rust
to the terminal dock

they hug close
like calf whales to a stricken cow
not about to let go
not about to let the tide
push them around

a shag sails down
skimming the eel grass
the glistening muck and plastic wrack
to land on a piling

watches as they nudge her in
holding fast
tending the gash in her side

even with her lashed tight
the tugs hang on

even with the job done
bobbing in a slick of oil

now the smaller one
glides slowly toward open water
spouting smoke

now
the others.

John Perrault

From Here

From here,
from Ceres Street,
Rush Realty, the Wine Merchant,
everything's the river
From Moran's
and Lindbergh's Crossing
—Don't even think of parking here—
the waves rise
then recede
they thrust, then pull
From Poco's Cantina
Salamandra
and the Bow Street Inn
"cozy," "unique"
a deep world sweeps by
its rippled back
baptizing tankers, draggers,
pleasure boats
From Harbour Place
and Morgan Stanley
and the Instinet that
covers every sector
every trend
the river swirls and eddies
clinging briefly
to the piers
of the Memorial Bridge
then hurtles on

Stfn Comack

We're All Tourists in Time

Time and Tide

In 1921 Grandpa piloted submarine 0-10
up the Piscataqua, submerged against the current
and the commander's orders
to arrive in time for my mother's birth
so I could sit in a row of professors
to watch *Koyaanisqatsi* flicker to a stop
in the Colonial Theater (now a parking lot).

David Watters

The Washington Step

My grandfather
had a red sandstone step
(once rough
worn round and smooth
by years of waiting, walking up and down)
outside his workshop.
The dandelions encircled it
in a friendly if obtrusive wreath.
He told me the story
of the step—
he was as proud of that rock slab
as he was of his father's saw—
it had once been outside the towering North Church,
when Portsmouth was a colonial seaport
and capital—
George Washington himself
once set foot upon it.
My mother laughed
at his whimsical history,
but I loved to lick
cold raspberry popsicles
on summer afternoons
while sitting on my grandfather's
little piece of history,
surrounded
by sunshine.

Megan Hamilton

Time Travel

Across the Piscataqua River
I linger on Market Street,
watch tourists hastily scurrying
from antique shops to toy stores.
The cry of a lone herring gull
as he swoops seaward
sharpens my senses,
focuses my attention
to a green mesh tower
of lobster traps patiently awaiting
tomorrow morning's toil. Two ruddy
faced fishermen inhale the frosty
November air, prepare their gear
for another early morning departure.

At Strawbery Banke
authentically clothed artisans
imitate the arduous workday
of eighteenth century craftsmen
while leisure tourists
cross the manicured grounds
in white, horse-drawn carriages.

In my daydreams
I am also swept away
in time.

Jim Brosnan

Strawbery Banke Roses and Dreams

My head is woolly
And full of fancies:
The old house above the shore
The scent of roses, pink
By the door, old door
Bull's eyed and raked
By asking claws
By briar straws
And then perhaps, who'd doubt?
By wolves
Or moon-touched forest gnomes
Who walked the woodland hereabout
When young sea roses grew
When the eyes of the bull were new.

Alda Irons

Strawbery Banke

The first of their days on shore
They fed on wild scarlet strawberries,
Surviving, and spreading their seed
Through generations of names
On ruined tombstones.
Here their houses have congregated
Patiently waiting
For the familiar spirits
Should they ever return
Looking for strawberries.

Laurel K. Walter

Players' Ring door

It was Either that or Starve

Pa was a big man,
Worked for the telephone company
setting poles.
But what he really liked
Was to go into the forest and cut down trees,
Chop wood,
But you don't make much of a living
Selling cords of wood.
There were eight of us.
Mother took in washing and ironing.

I grew up on a farm down off Lafayette
We had animals, a chicken coop, big garden, pigs,
We lived off the fat of the land,
But, oh, we were poor.

We'd go down to the edge of town
Look for things to play with,
Made sleds out of pasteboard boxes,
Had fun sliding down the hills.

I went to St. Pat's,
And we walked four times a day.
When it was bad weather,
We hopped a pung.

Mother was a pussy cat.
I hated to go to school,
I didn't have pretty clothes.
I'd say, "Ma, I have a headache."
She'd say, "Lie down, dear,
I'll make you a nice cup of tea"
(I never had a headache in my life).

Ann Sadler (as told to Anne Dewees)

A Story of Silence (at Goodwin Park)

My wife returns
from her evening walk,
and tells me a story
of silence:

You enter the park
and are surrounded by roads,
but there is no traffic.

Clouds are above you,
but there is no wind.

You remember
a century ago,
citizens gathered
at this stone memorial
to soldier and sailor,
cheering the explosion
of gunshot and fireworks.

Starlings and sparrows
hid in the trees.

You are what happens next.

You are those unheard
voices in houses nearby.

You are the children
riding their bicycles.

You are the pleasure of flowers,
the caterpillar beneath the small rock.

You are the space between branches.

You are the song
in the throat
of the tiniest bird,
before the song
has been sung.

W.E. Butts

Great Expectations: Wentworth-by-the-Sea

On a soiled linen tablecloth of old snow
sits Miss Havisham's wedding cake,
this abandoned summer hotel.

Its peeling white paint is rotted frosting.
Its gaping windows, mouse holes.
The Victorian fretworks topping its mansard towers
are beetle-eaten sugar roses.
    "A great cake. A bride cake."

The partying has long been over.
The promised bridegroom
never appeared.
All the guests, vanished.

A spark to a tattered wedding gown—
    I saw a great flaming light spring up...
    a whirl of fire blazing...
Will you burn, Wentworth?

Or will the tardy bridegroom come
in his shining carriage,
restart the stopped clocks,
make everything fresh and bright,
let in the new day,
fulfill at last our great expectations?

Pat Parnell

Wentworth-by-the-Sea

Portsmouth Hurt

I'll tell you about my home —
The place where I was born.
I traveled, lived, not roamed
With artists of brush, pen and song.

You'll want to know about the trees.
The ones along Maplewood Ave.
They bordered Portsmouth with their leaves,
Yet were cut, destroyed, and roots stabbed.

And what about the White Birches
At the plaza there?
Trees removed after torture –
The parking lot left bare!

What about the South End?
Our favorite Puddle Dock?
Out-of-staters moved in;
Renovating to beat the clock.

What about the lobsters
Of Portsmouth and the coast?
Stolen from their homes by mobsters
Who boil them alive for a clambake roast.

When I came back the birds were gone,
Killed by hunters galore.
Leaving us only to hear the song
Of gulls and pigeons on the shore.

The majestic tree growth along the way
From Portsmouth to Newington gone!
Into extinction one sad day;
Not even yet remembered in a song!

Suzy "Courage" Johnson

At the Athenæum

The milling crowd in Market Square
lets them through this time,
the resolute matrons
with their platters of strawberries,
cucumber sandwiches.

Upstairs it is festive.
Guests refill their wine glasses,
File through a sage green gallery.
They contemplate

Encased botanical sketch books,
hand painted teacups,
pimpernel pattern,
butterfly handles.

They pay homage
to pages of poetry
embellished with pansies,
the work of a woman
who lived near this town
a hundred years ago.

Below, the Saturday night crowd
contemplates navel jewelry,
watches for Harleys,
turns up the volume.

The clock on North Church steeple
chimes eight.
The midsummer light persists.
"Primrose, pimpernel, big deal."

Janice Warren

The Athenæum

The Athenæum

Filtered through the double-arched elegance
of the august and ancient windows
the white blast of twenty-first century sun
is dimmed to mellow nineteenth century gold.

The draped-shouldered busts of romanticized-in-death
past state governors and founders of this fine
establishment peer down in shiny sternness
through the dust-churned shafts, waiting

while the heavy table – striped with layered
periodicals – painted chairs, wooden cane stands
and glass cases contemplate in studied silence
their next slow move across the chequer-board floor.

Upstairs in the library proper, where sea charts hang
and sections of whale vertebrae thick as tree trunks
rest upon the deep, slate-lined window sills,
the ghosts of tides pass back and forth.

The far off cries of gulls, rhythmic tread of waves
the wavering lines of men's lives at sea
are condensed into the quietness of words
in whose grey-lined steadiness the past –

no longer ordained but chosen – loses its pain
and can be read at will or random over again,
distilled, transpired, exhaled into the faintest breath of spray
rising on air currents, falling with the dust.

Diana Durham

Peverly Hill

From Sagamore Creek to Peverly's Hill
Thomas Peverly settled early on.
A house he built quite near the Creek
and with Jane Walford settled down.

And through the years he gave his all
surveying land around.
He reared up children to be good,
to abide by tenets sound.

There were no wide paved highways,
no bridges to cross the creek,
just up South Road and through the Plains
to Peverly Hill Road each week.

And even today in nearby towns
some Peverlys still reside,
though for many years they've traveled
to other states far and wide.

And sometimes they drive along that hill
or stop by Sagamore Creek,
and think of earlier Portsmouth folk
and wish that they could speak.

To talk about those days long gone,
when few men lived around,
these men who gave their all back then
to this special Portsmouth town.

Elaine M. Peverly

History Room (Portsmouth Public Library)
Shakespeare said, *There's rosemary. That's for remembrance.*

With cream white walls, pumpkin carpet
in almost squareness, a laughing Buddha
electric magic on pages known by candles
the room is plum for the seacoast historian
afternoon browser, genealogist and scholar.
Expect no lock no key no window no hip
rock tunes no cheese or tuna sandwiches.
Order gives shape to abundance – history
cramped in envelopes, breathless volumes
plastic and marbled jackets, sea blue paper
fine grain cinnamon leathers, archived linen
thinner than a bookish mouse. Tea brown
news pasted side-by-side tea brown picnics
family tomes, spined tall and firm and sure,
glad company to weary neighbors. Facts on
imports and immigrants, fishing folk, farmers
philanthropists, men named Mason, Jackson
Cutts, Wentworth, Lane, whalers and sailors
Seavey, Whipple, Sherburne and more...
aristocrats, rebels, haberdashers, preachers
births-deaths-marriages catalogued, servants
slaves and women, yes – widows of the sea
midwives, weavers, elegance and homespun.
Index files, one go-round clock, three lean chairs
stub pencils, no erasers, a murder shackled to fame
cheers for tavern keepers, pomp and liberation
cummerbunds and treaties, paper tales to dazzle.
In this room not set to sleep, we are the tapestry.
Sign a small register, the fragrance is rosemary.

Julie Abbott Mulloy

Ghosts of the Temple

Slave ghosts on the cobblestones,
Colonial ghosts in the windows,
They all line the streets
And watch.

Sometimes they follow me into
The soup place
Or the toast place,
But keep away from the dolphin place
Where the napkins are rumored to be cloth.

But when I feel them
On the steps of the temple,
It's there that they
invite me in.

Jeanne M. Krasnansky

Gravestones

The Proprietors' Burial Ground

A wrought iron gate opens wide,
the road circles round
a nearly perfect pond.
Its still surface reflects
the autumn red and gold of trees
more clearly than the real
but upside down – not unlike
the memory of an unexpected death.
An egret, elegant in silhouette,
walks carefully
on stilted legs,
his long-necked head darts
forward for a fish.
All around the silent stones,
beyond the sea
lapping at the shore,
depositing small shells
as seasons come and go,
come and go.

Terry Karnan

Portsmouth Poseidon

the widows' walk atop
Olde-century manses,
It's said where women
Watched and waited long
for husbands to return
from the omnipotent sea
and
fewer ever did than not

and those who knew futility
and did not leap
in grief to oblivion
were endowed
by the powers of the sea
with the will and strength
to forge a new life
from the rusted anchors
of the lost and olde,
Sunken beams to resuscitate

and the ghosts of all
Galleys' bell to sound
in choir a new melody
Abubble with Wagnerian triumph

Charlene Mary-Cath Smith

The Old Neighborhood

Of course, the old Puddledock neighborhood is gone. Mostly where
Strawbery Banke is now is where I grew up. During high school,
I worked at J.J. Newberry's right in Market Square, '49, '50.
Downstairs, they sold birds, fish, material, house wares, aprons,
that's where I was. I loved it there. So many of the old stores are
gone now too. We used to go to Bratter's Bakery, where you
walked in on a wooden walkway. The floor was always covered in
flour. They made the best cinnamon rolls. And Montgomery
Wards, across from Hudsons, now. The floors were so old they
used to creak. We didn't have refrigeration in those days, so we
shopped for food almost every day. We'd put a card in the win-
dow ICE, and the iceman, he would walk right in and put the ice
in the icebox. We never locked the doors. On Saturdays, I would
do the shopping for Mother. I'd go up to Emil's Meat Market,
then Sher's Bakery, and then the First National Store, for beans
and hot dogs. All those stores are gone now. Paul's Market, they
delivered groceries, was on Daniel Street, where Carlson's Travel
Agency is now. Emil's was where the Dolphin Striker is, the First
National Store right across from the old Post Office and Abbott's,
which is in Strawbery Banke. We hung out a lot at the Victory
Spa. They had the most wonderful sodas. Then there was
McNabbs and Georgie Gould's on Charles Street. Georgie's was
kind of rough and tough, but she sold penny candy. The men
would sit on the cooler or pitch horseshoes in the empty field next
door. At supper time, Mother would say, "Go down to Georgie's
and get Father." The Badger Creamery was where St. John's
parking lot is now. Here's our 1982 Puddledock Reunion Book –
such a close knit neighborhood it was. Here's the picture of the
Liberty Bridge Laundry Gang and here's some of the kids sitting
in front of four bear skins hung up on the fence.

Joan M. Alessi (as told to Anne Dewees)

Salt piles

Inside the Berbar-greene

dedicated to Dave Mahoney, Armand LaCasse, Joe Putnam, Mike
   Patterson, Willie King, John Dumkowski, Dave Geary, Gene
   Brown and others.

In '76 I worked those white mountains by the sea,
with dry, dusty, rock salt from Chile,
the sea salt from Spain and Portugal,
and the ochre shaded salt of Ireland.

We scooped it up in machines with buckets
like five yard maws.
And dumped it in the berbar-greene,
where it went into an inverted pyramid,
whose truncated tip had an oscillating shuttle,
then a long conveyor belt,
agitating into piles of respectable salt and
tailings of smaller clumps,
and before we shut it down we'd clean the machine,
so caked and crusted salt couldn't harden overnight.

This day, I gave the high sign to Mike to dump his last load;
John was scuttling across the yard to the garage like a giant yellow crab,
so I figured he was probably done.
Up I go inside with the shovel poised,
descending into the depths
until I'm riding back and forth like on a rocking ship.

But something's wrong; salt comes down.
It's raining tons of salt!
John's come back to dump one last load.

Oh, stop, please!, the salt is to my knees —
the salt keeps pouring in; it's at my waist, now at my chin.
I wave and shout, "I'm inside the berbar-greene!"

Donald R. Young

Gilley's

Gilley's

Oh, if only these walls could talk
what an interesting story they'd tell
of this City by the sea
and the folks who know it so well.

The stools have seen hunger
and probably gluttony too –
the well-dressed professor
and the tramps passing through.

These walls enclose a forum
of local politics and sports –
of the Celtics and the Bruins
and Red Sox spring training reports.

Each evening to the square
where it stayed for most of the night.
These walls show wear from years of use,
and scars from an occasional fight.

"Two with the works", I hear echo.
The walls seem to ring with the cry –
dogs with mustard, relish and onion
as quick as hands could fly.

Just simple fare, but hearty –
no fancy menus here.
Top it off with black coffee
to settle the evening's beer.

Oh, the sands of time pass onward
and the old place sees new clerks,
but, just listen and you'll still hear –
"Gilley, make it two more with the works!"

Fred Pettigrew

For Fifteen Cents You Had It All

In the late 1930s and early 1940s, Portsmouth had three movie theaters. First, the Colonial, now part of Eagle Photo on Congress Street, which showed all the A movies with stars like Clark Gable, Myrna Loy, Bette Davis, and Errol Flynn. The movies changed three times a week and they were continuous. If you sat there, you could see them twice. I remember on a Sunday night, you would see everyone you knew at the Colonial. If the movie was good, the line would go right around North Church. In 1938, our family saw the opening of *Gone with the Wind*. That was a gala evening. It was a four hour movie, the seats were more expensive, AND I was one of the only children there.

The Olympia Theater on Vaughn Street, now the Vaughn Street Mall, showed B movies and foreign films. You saw two movies for the price of admission. You could spend half a day there. I remember during the war an English movie called *One of Our Aircraft is Missing*.

We'd walk to the Acadia Theater in the Franklin Block, where Choozy Shoes is now, on the Congress Street side. There was a long flight of stairs; you'd buy your ticket at the bottom, then climb up one flight. It was nicknamed the Scratch House, kind of dingy, the sound equipment wasn't very good. It usually showed the C movies, cowboy films made by Republic Studio, starring Gene Autry, Roy Rogers and the Sons of the Pioneers, and comedies with the Three Stooges. Children ten cents, five cents for a chocolate bar with almonds which I bought before I went in. For fifteen cents, you had it all. Every week, my grandmother went to the Acadia. It wasn't just because she loved cowboys films, she went because each person received a dish or a plate with the price of admission. My grandfather always accompanied her, and when I was available, so did I; then it was a "three dish day."

Elaine Shapiro Krasker (as told to Anne Dewees and Mimi White)

In the Neighborhood

You have to live twenty years in a place to claim
never to have been there. Before that you're not quite sure.
There are everywheres everywhere.
A moment of shared laughter, a scent of new-cut grass
will give strangeness a familiar face.

Yet if my heart has a true home
it lies in ruins where people are foolishly
building anew. Where even now in the rubble
someone is clearing a path, and a sheet of transparent
plastic catches the wind like a guiltless flag.

Robert Dunn

Bench on Four Tree Island

Four Tree Island

Wake up on Islington
Neighbor plays guitar
Read paper, hum along
Grab favorite book and go
Peer at reflection in Bread Box glass
Hear Billie Holliday by heart-shaped lamps
Slouch with guilt by health food store
Look with longing where Little Professor taught
Order the regular at Breaking New Grounds
Tip-toe through the tourists at Brioche
Eavesdrop past the Kilim debates
Smile at Harry Potter in Shoofly Pie window
Act as tour guide down State Street
Zig zag through runners over bridge to Peirce Island
Slip through the iron gates
To my sometime private island
Follow long path of stones
Escape with Tolkien, Orwell, King
Listen to music of seagulls
Sip coffee and drink in the memories of Home.

Gina Carbone

Progress

A city whose skyline has changed.
Brown air dripping droplets
Ozone heavy on highrises.
The fog rolls in from the West.
Golden Gates shrouded; fog horns in the night.

The city is here. Tugboats, tourists, and trolleys.
A town whose landscape is changing.
Diamond interchanges in DSL lanes,
Parking garages, and traffic.
Fog banks in the east,
The Isles of Shoals appear the way they were.

The sea is still in fog,
Lobster is not the Dungeness Crab.
I walk these streets,
A visitor to memory, a resident to change.

Vic Richards

Returning to the Coast

Meadows are alive with crickets,
Red-winged Blackbirds balance on cattails
rustling above the sea-grass marsh.
A setting half moon tints the sloping pasture.
Deer graze in the bog. A Great Blue Heron,
thin, graceful, glides low over the horizon.
My spirit glides with it.

I follow the familiar road to where an owl might rise
from the march of extravagant sugar maples
bordering my yard. The narrative of this old house,
surrounded by climbing roses, deep purple lilacs,
and Lilies-of-the-valley,
welcomes me.

I hear stories in the hand-hewn beams,
and pumpkin pine floors, the beehive fireplace
and my life begins again,
roots replanted in rich soil,
back where they belong.

Julie Bigg Veazey

Tide pool

November

late afternoon chill,
tide dead low
a slash of silver
disjoins gray sea from sky

brown rockweed tracings
on hard packed sand,
I search gleaming
tide pool mirrors for answers

Anne Dewees

The Mourning Dove
(Pocket Gardens, Portsmouth, NH)

Early evening. June.
The ladies on the garden tour
admire the floral border freshened by rain
in a small back yard in this small city.

Over the arbor,
wisteria blooms in a tangle.

Only inches away, on her nest
the mourning dove holds herself tight and still.
Her bright unblinking eye looks strained.

How hard it is
to be invisible in this world.

Elizabeth Knies

In the South End

Crossing the fifth bridge
one saw seven egrets
standing in the mud
of the South Mill Pond
where it began hereabouts.

Though one might be tempted
to do things with the birds
and the mud—the fair needs
foul sort of thing—or
to push the numbers hard,
the fact is the egrets were
and are the thing that needs
no doing, north or south,
then or now. The whiteness
was and is indeed enough.

Hugh Hennedy

Urban Heron: Portsmouth, New Hampshire

The heron ankle deep in the pond —
it's not clear till the interruption,

till something fetches its eye and turns
its neck one tenth of a wring —

that this is not someone's
misplaced lawn furniture.

I don't even notice its upside down shadow
for minutes, an adaptation

of the urban heron. I'm thinking
of all the stove-in mailboxes

in a ten-mile radius of the pond
and how Father Nash drove his altar boys

around at night shooting up
anything that was a *sign*.

I replaced ours with a new Sears box,
missing some washers and the ability to mount.

So mom waves in Louie, from across the street
and Iwo Jima, who dismantles my mailbox,

replaces the Japanese imperfecta
with titanium from Sikorsky Helicopters,

that would outlive my mother's shrine
and waver no more than the heron

or the imitating couple doing Tai Chi,
graceful, despite the human slips, the imbalance,

and what I love is the way
it ends — he turns, she turns,

they face and lock fingers at pocket level,
their hands swing up and they fall

into an embrace, splay-fingered and toed,
stumble apart, but it's not clear till she slaps him

on the back, almost slapstick,
almost applauding,

that the heron has vanished.

Kevin King

Flying over Portsmouth

As I stride out of my Portsmouth home,
I tiptoe through the damp grass.
I reach my trampoline and clamber on.
I fire up over and over again.
Sometimes I feel like I am soaring through the
air into outer space.
I suck in the clean, crisp air like a vacuum cleaner
then I let it out.
Suddenly my feet start to ache.
I groan and look down realizing that I HAVE to
sweep again.
After flying over the trampoline for a while,
I fall to the black surface, out of breath.
I see beautiful clouds, hanging out in the sky.
I can also feel the trees vibrating against each other
as their leaves hover to the ground.
I stride back to my Portsmouth home.

Maggie O'Brien

Woodbury Avenue

Accidental Light

All the way home along Woodbury Avenue,
words for light explode
in my mouth like cold green grapes:
 lucent   *luminous*
I'm eleven, and I've just discovered the thesaurus:
the words like paths
leading off from one main road, like lives
all beginning in the same body.

There is no schoolbus stop,
so the driver pulls close to a slope of snow
piled up against a telephone pole. As I jump
from the bus to the slippery heap,
the closing doors nip my heel.

I slip, and think I feel
the crunch of wheels across my heart.
Is it only fear that flares
    luminescent
in my chest? When the bus pulls away
up the narrow white road, I don't know
if I've fallen beneath its wheels and died,

or if I'm standing in some other life,
on some other road home.
All my life I will remember this
as the day I know there is more
than one universe, or maybe
no such thing as this one. I keep looking

at the oatmeal slush around my feet,
then down the road to where our distant
kitchen windows shimmer, orange
in the setting sun.
    incandescent.
But I might not be alive. I feel my head
itch beneath the woolly stocking cap,
hear tinkling voices
    radiant   *lustrous*
tell me I can choose – right now.

Behind me
there might be a body in the road. People
might be gathering, deciding who will go
to tell my mother. But I don't look back.
I remember there are stars

on my bedroom ceiling that glow in the dark,
    phosphorescent
and decide not to be dead. Decide to live
a long and ignorant life, to start now
toward home.

Katherine E. Solomon

Three Moons

"Full moon! Oh, you must
Go see it, now! You know
The golden hugeness changes soon."

Where to go? I love the trees
Near my house; they're full of stories,
But allow no view of newly rising
September lunar glory.

Aha! Into the car
And onto the bypass!
The bridge is empty,
Free of traffic, lucky me.
While paying strict attention
To the road, of course,
I creep along and catch the view.
Too soon I'm now in Maine.
Oh, I need to turn;
Quick! Back to Portsmouth
On the Memorial Bridge!

Another moon-on-water,
Trailing gold like a shimmering kite-tail.
Not enough! Need more!
The show's not over yet!
Quick, around the block,
Left on State,
Slide sedately into Prescott Park.

There! Still golden!
Still huge! Hanging there,
Letting the gold pour down,
Like water pouring off a
Weighing anchor,
Rising higher through the swaying masts,
As though through waving grasses.

In the quiet, I begin to notice
The slow activity: the dog walkers;
The strollers, arm in arm;
The other moon watcher.
A man with two full grocery bags.
As I watch, he passes,
Toward the dock,
And disappears. Until I see
The cabin light go on,
And he is home.

Mary Gildea

A Night on the Town

Weekend.
Time of homework.
Promised my mom that if she comes over,
She'll help me study,
She is my best friend.
When she comes over, we spruce ourselves up for a night on the town.
I'm frozen.
I'm wearing a tee-shirt and it's a chilly night in October.
Before we get to the little green bridge,
She stops and looks across the water.
Staring at the lights on the skyline,
She says, "Would you look at that?
We live in a postcard!"
I agree.
I remember when there were friendly old men
Who would say hello to anyone passing by.
Now, when I walk past
I could say Good Morning to the roadblocks,
But I don't bother.
We finally arrive in town.
It's Saturday night,
But it's October—not July
So there are few people out and about.
Had planned on getting warm in a cozy coffeehouse.
I get a sudden urge for ice cream
And there's a change of plans.
On the way to satisfy my craving,
We bump into another friend,
Who was wandering around
Looking for someone to bump into.
After ice cream,
And being frozen,
Me and the original she walk back home
Arm in arm to keep warm.
Time for homework.
Weekend.

Camille Rose Perrin

Beauty Lives

She floats in and out
of blue specter's palette,
her cool skeleton hand
holds mine, warm and peach-tan.

Milli's lids flutter
as Fred reads his poems to her.
We lean into her white bedspread,
sheets, face, and hair.

Through the picture window
sun pours golden shine
on the butterfly and lily field
in Milli's painting. Her canvas,
spring on the sick room's wall.

Outside Wentworth Home,
Pleasant Street this October
belies the growing season
has passed. Bright pink flowers spike
still summer skies blushed salmon.

The afternoon rests
in high bloom
splendor, as we reminisce
on the bench at Prescott Park.

In my mind's eye, Milli
dances, tiny octogenarian
in teal green sweat suit
sprightly she gardens,
creates art, ever recreates.

At the ocean's view,
beauty wings on the sea breeze.
A monarch, lone migrator,
alights on the last marigold.

Karen Galipeau

Toys R Us

Toys piled high, towering above
On shelves that reach the sky.
You won't be able to walk in and out and not
See something you can't do without.

Right across the street from my home, it's

Unbelievable that I live
So close to a toy store as large as Ancient Rome.

Brian Smith

Toys R Us

Where I Live

My street is busy, just like me.
It is always loud, just like me.
It is full of life, just like me.
But, at night, it is peaceful and quiet,
just like me.

Tanisha Noyes

613 Union Street

Did I tell you how they used to block off Union Street from South
Street to Lincoln Avenue for coasting every winter? We'd slide
down the hill and then drag our feet to turn onto Hawthorne. We
had a wonderful time. The boys would bring bobsleds; only boys
could ride them except if they liked a girl, they'd ask her. I never
got asked. Then they'd all come back to our house for cocoa and
ping-pong. Our house was the meeting place. The house was
always full, Mother and Dad might be having a party upstairs
and we'd be in the playroom with our friends. Once I remember a
neighbor spread ashes out on the street. Of course, then we
couldn't slide down. I remember Father put on his overcoat and
marched over, knocked on the door and said, "Don't you ever do
that again. Now you get out there and help those kids shovel the
snow back on to that street." I coasted there all through junior
high and high school and even on vacations when I came home
from college.

Frances R. Snook (as told to Anne Dewees and Mimi White)

After High School

To you, this town was old;
junky with back alleys, and the weeds pushing tall under us.

When you took me dancing, the curve of you
set something under me, and those little-girl days
of you chasing fireflies waved us good-bye.

You never thought of sowing rows of steam
into the seams of me, but there it is.

The town looked different to me then, and the
rows of buildings smiled at me when I raced
through the streets.

Nobody really knows this, but I used to love this town
because of you. Yeah, it was old, but honey I know
about your tall buildings and the dreams nobody wants.

I wanted to keep it all for you. This town.
This town might just let me. But the angel
in my taxi won't let me forget my friends
are waiting for me again.

There's enough back roads here
for the both of us. You stay in that window,
and I'll dance under it.

James Kimble

760 State

In bed alone that first night
switching the light off
a sky miraculously appears

stars in too perfect constellations
—I can't imagine
what is happening

floating in a small bedroom
on the top floor of a red wooden house
across from an overgrown park

newly divorced, back in a city
a city where I can walk & walk
to Karen's...to South Pond...

to the hospital where my son was born
to jazz at the Press Room
(jazz my consolation, my hopeful song!)

to Cafe Petronella...to Luka's...
down to the river through the park
and the gardens (old growth withering)

circling back through town
walking, figuring, walking
walking into a new life.

Harvey Shepard

Portsmouth's Queen Anne Houses

Seated majestically on their lots,
Well back from Middle Street,
Smilingly sure of their superior worth.
Just think of the money they cost!
The Queen Anne houses.

Not the Queen Anne the Brits call to mind,
But the American design of the Queen.
These ladies proclaim their power and prestige,
Totally sure they're top of the class.

Broad steps lead up to the porches,
Big porches girdle their fronts.
Full curves are part of their frontage,
Their skirts are flung very wide.

Deep colored paint on the ground floor exterior,
Lighter colors on the shingles above,
Two stories of windows raise the eye to a turret
Roof lines jut out at odd angles,
Oh blissful abundant life.

They're buxom, they're brash and they're lovely,
The Queen Anne houses.

Marjorie Dannis

Portsmouth Queen Anne house

Achy Morns in Winter

Achy morns in Winter;
Watching the cold Cat –
Frigid-faced, itchy hands, wet toes –
Scratch and rub life anew
To his whiskers while
Whistling whimsically down cobblestone sidewalks,
In an ancient New England town
Where the ocean's fragrance
Tip-toes reticently under his nose.
Naked seedlings careen in front of village shops,
As proprietors sweep the pure white drifts
That lie in heaps at their door,
Before bustling patrons respond to the
Nine chimes echoing from the clock,
Nestled in a church's tower.
Blues, reds, and yellows adorn the crisp sky
Yielding a soft wind that sings a song
Of yesterday's Fall symphony.
Snow-covered benches welcome
Indolent old men with icicles clinging to their beards,
Regarding life with a genial grin,
As ivory figures pass through
On achy morns in Winter.

Nathan J. Belanger

Through My Window

Through my window there's a whole New World.

I see leaves falling off bare trees but my birth tree
stands strong.

The grass is light green like the green you see in
seaweed after a storm.

I look at the water. It is so calm and quiet you can hear
a leaf hit the water's glassy surface.

I hear dogs barking and children laughing and playing.

Then the day comes to an end and I watch the sun set
over the horizon through my window.

Nick Foster

Meadowbrook Fields

The wonderful Portsmouth sun glares on a creek nearby.
Small newborn grasshoppers and beetles crawl in the
meadows thinking they're in a safari jungle.
They look around but nothing's there, then suddenly
Animal Control speeds in and snatches the coyote with rabies.
The people in the Meadowbrook Inn stand and look on in awe.
The circle of life.

Adam Studer

Terminus (for Jon Guilbert)

The empty railtracks gleam ahead of us
unused now, as we walk on the sleepers
like stepping stones of wood through the shadows.
You know it with your trainspotting eye:
this line used to go down to Boston
and all the way up to Maine
and we wonder where we are going...

We've come out into the twilight
two thirsty, intellectual men
into the suburban night of America
stretching as far as the eye can see
hovering like a moth at the flame of its emptiness,
that is the night of the world too, in its rottenness
and on its knees

And I'm saying we need something
that is not of this world
even as we are within it
that can't be counted, bought or sold,
and I'm making a circle with both my hands
a *temenos* of stretched fingers in front of my heart
as fragile as a sandcastle to the incoming tide
and in as much need of maintaining...

A sacred circle that is who we love, too
that is family, with our children (if we have them)
otherwise, my friend, we get slowly eaten alive
till all that's left in us is what is outside us
like black soot filling our cells
reaching like these tracks, nowhere ahead
as we come to their terminus
where the buffer once stood

pausing for a moment, disoriented
our steps wavering in the darkness
at this End that is exactly where we are...

before we cut across the late streets to the bar
to douse the pain with darts and beer,
or use it as skillful respite

returning to the inner press and forge
of our realer lives.

Jay Ramsay

Portsmouth Unabridged

We map out a bright welcome of nouns –
steeple, square,
parking garage, park, peaveys,
brioche, hammer, moe, toast.

Then Piscataqua, our long local verb,
flows, rushes, silvers, boat-dances, bridges.

We preposition the past –
when submarines, where strawberries,
before Goodwin Park, Naval Prison,
beneath Star, salt piles.

We discover that neighborhoods
are all about conjunction –
nine or ninety years old,
native or newcomer,
pocket garden or washington step,
queen anne house or dragon crane,
and the all-important "but"
mentioned by poet Adrian,
page twenty, "This town harbors
what we need to carry on. Difference."
Finally – and, and, and,
one after another,
we poets write this crazy and—ology –
new poems, old city,
and
tomorrow ...

Maren C. Tirabassi

Arrival

I arrived
a strange man from a strange land.
Foreign to the faces
that walked along Market Street and sat at the cafés.
Foreign to the faces
of the tall white steeple,
the red brick buildings
and the wooden homes of yore.
Foreign to the faces
of the three tall bridges
that grow in stature from East to West.
Foreign to the face
that was reflected back to me
as I stared at the river flowing by.
I looked up and wondered who I was,
where I was,
and why.
I looked back across my new town,
breathed in the fresh salty air,
and the tasty scents from the kitchens scattered throughout
Portsmouth,
and my answer came.
I was finally home.
I arrived where I was meant to be.

Michael Wesley McKenna

About the Editor

Maren C. Tirabassi is the Poet Laureate of Portsmouth from 2001-2003. Recent books of poetry are *The Depth of Wells* and *Faith Made Visible*. As a liturgical writer for Pilgrim Press, her earlier books are *Blessing New Voices* (an anthology of prayers and poems by adolescents), *An Improbable Gift of Blessing*, *Gifts Of Many Cultures*, and *Touch Holiness*. Maren teaches the writing of poetry and memoir in schools and prisons, is the pastor of Northwood Congregational United Church of Christ and travels as a frequent speaker and workshop leader for interfaith conferences throughout the United States.

Originally from Iowa, Maren has degrees from Carlton College, Northfield, Minnesota, Union Theological Seminary, New York and Harvard Divinity School. She and her family moved to Portsmouth in 1992.

About the Photographer

With just a decade on the Seacoast, Richard Haynes says he originally migrated from South Carolina to New York City. At the age of nine he saw his first movie there, *Ben Hur* and fell in love with the camera. A junior high school teacher steered him also toward painting and he entered the High School of Art and Design in 1965. After the Air Force he earned his BFA. Richard received an MFA in Photography from Pratt Institute. He worked his way up through the ranks at Holt, Rhinehart & Winston, and eventually turned to freelance work. His clients now include Houghton-Mifflin, Prentice-Hall, and Oxford University Press. Besides his photography, Richard is also an accomplished painter. Today he lives with his wife and family in Portsmouth, New Hampshire.